Gemma goes for a short stay in the countryside with her gran and when her parents arrive to collect her, they have a pleasant surprise.

STEPHEN RUSSELL

PICKING DAISIES

ILLUSTRATED BY SARA FLOYD

AUSTIN MACAULEY PUBLISHERS™
LONDON • CAMBRIDGE • NEW YORK • SHARJAH

A CIP catalogue record for this title is available from the British Library.

ISBN 9781528918985 (Paperback)
ISBN 9781528962520 (ePub e-book)

www.austinmacauley.com

First Published 2024
Austin Macauley Publishers Ltd®
1 Canada Square
Canary Wharf
London
E14 5AA

I would like to dedicate this book to my two grandmothers and my parents who introduced me to the wonderful world of storytelling.

–Stephen Russell

For my parents, Allan and Angela Coulson, for always believing in me.

–Sara Floyd

The little girl picked a daisy from the lawn and added it to the rest. She was pleased at the chain she had made from
her favourite flower.

"Gemma, we're leaving for Gran's now."

"Coming," she replied, eager to show her mum what she'd made.

When Gemma went into the house, she held the daisy chain out to her mum and said, "Look what I made for you."

"Aw, Gemma, sweetheart, that's beautiful."

As Gemma sat in the back of her dad's car, she was excited at the thought of staying with her gran, who lived in the country, with a house that was great to visit. It smelled of the flowers that grew in her garden. It was a place that Gemma loved; the colours and smells. The garden was filled with flowers which her gran grew herself from seed. She kept them in her special cupboard with tiny little drawers for each type of flower, which was in the potting shedin the corner of the garden.

Salva
Phlox
Violet
Jasmin
Daisies
Rose
Dahlia
Peony
Hydran
Poppy
Aster
Begonia
Irises
Freesia
Petunia
Clematis

Gemma looked out of the window as her dad's car edged out of the town
and into the countryside.
"Look at the lambs playing," she said excitedly, unwrapping the sweet her
mum had just given her.
"Look, Gemma, it's the windmill," said her dad.
"Yay, we're near gran's house!"

VIM 474

Pretty soon the house came into view, and no sooner had her dad parked the car and opened her door, Gemma jumped out and dashed towards it. The front door opened and Gemma flung herself into her gran's arms.

"Hello, poppet," said a smiling Gran. "You'll soon be taller than me."

Gemma went into the house and heard her dad say they were running late for a hospital appointment. When her gran came into the house, Gemma asked why her parents were going to the hospital.

"Nothing for you to worry about," replied her gran with a beaming smile. "I've got plenty to show you in the garden, but first we're going to have some bread and honey for tea."

Afterwards, Gran asked Gemma if she remembered about helping plant seeds on her last visit. "Let's go into the garden," said Gran as she reached out her hand. They both went outside to work and to play, and Gemma stood, her eyes wide as saucers.

"Look at all the pretty colours," she squealed excitedly.

Gran gave a hearty chuckle and walked Gemma through the garden and started telling her about each of the different types of flowers. "Those small purple ones with the yellow centre are crocuses," said Gran. "And those big pink flowers are dahlias," Gemma listened and laughed at some of the names. She heard names like foxglove, lilies, poppies and tulips, and marvelled at the rainbow of bright colours, then she spotted something. Beside the roses, which she knew without Gran's help, Gemma got really excited.

After breakfast, Gemma got washed up quickly, dressed and went downstairs. She found that Gran had already gone outside and she hurried on out to join her.

"I'm just planting a couple of new plants," said Gran, as Gemma crouched beside her. "Your mum and dad will be here soon," she said, getting to her feet. "Are you going to help me pick some nice flowers for your mum?"
"Can I water the rest after that, Gran?"
"Of course you can," knowing that her granddaughter loved spraying the water. So they picked crocus, dahlias, daisies, roses and tulips. Gran formed them into a nice bunch as Gemma happily watered the rest.
Before supper, they had watered all the flowers in the garden, and Gemma was pleased that Gran had allowed her to use the hose. Later, as Gemma sat at the table facing gran, she asked her what her favourite flower was.
"Pansies, what about yours, poppet?" replied Gran.

"Bless us all," said a surprised Gran. "Time for bed, young lady."

"Can I not stay up a bit longer?" asked Gemma.

"Okay, you rascal, another ten minutes," said Gran, shaking her head.

Gemma asked about the tall yellow flowers in the big pots at the bottom of the garden.

"They're sunflowers," Gran told her. "They are one of the tallest of all flowers.

"Now time for bed, poppet," said Gran. "I want you to help me tomorrow in the garden before your mum and dad arrive."

"Do you want me to water the flowers again?" asked Gemma.

"Yes, that would be a great help," replied Gran.

After Gemma had brushed her teeth and climbed into bed, she said to her Gran, "I wish we had a garden like yours."

"You will someday, sweet dreams," sighed Gran. She smiled as she kissed her goodnight.

"Goodnight, Gran, love you lots," said a very sleepy Gemma.

It was the early morning sun peeping through the curtains that woke Gemma. Yawning, she sat up in bed and gave a big stretch before she climbed out onto the floor. As she came down the stairs, she could hear Gran singing in the kitchen.

"Morning, Gran," said Gemma, as she walked into the kitchen. She noticed the table, and on it was a bowl of her favourite cereal, already prepared, and a jug of cold milk along with honey and jam and a batch of Gran's homemade bread.

"When we have had breakfast, we can go into the garden," said Gran, as
she filled her teapot with hot water.
Gemma was excited about more time surrounded by the beautiful petals,
leaves, grass and colours of the garden.
***

She'd just sat the hose down when Gran told her that her mum and dad
were here.
Gemma went into the house and smiled as she ran to give
her mum a hug.
As she hugged her dad, Gemma looked up at him saying, "I've had such a
lovely time in the garden."
Gran walked in from the kitchen with a tray and gave Gemma a glass of
lemonade, before her dad asked her to sit down.
"We got good news at the hospital yesterday," he said.
Looking at Gemma, he told her that she was soon going to have
a little sister.

"Yay!" cried Gemma with a huge smile on her face.
The months passed and Gemma visited her Gran many more times, and
helped her plant more seeds to make the garden pretty in
the springtime.
When her mum was taken into the hospital, Gran came to stay with her.
She had lots of pots with flowers in them, and over the next few days
planted them with Gemma in Gemma's own garden.

When they had finished, Gran said, "I told you that you would have a
pretty garden someday, poppet."

Gemma hugged her and told her that she was the best Gran in the
world. Gemma picked some flowers for her mum.
A gift for later.
Her dad came out to the garden and said that he had a surprise for
them both.
Gemma asked what the surprise was, but was taken out to the car
without being told. Her dad said that she'd find out soon enough.

They turned into the hospital and parked outside in the carp park. As
they walked up the corridor of the baby unit, her dad gestured to a side
room and said, "In there." Gemma saw her mum with her new sister. She
went over and after giving her mum the flowers she had brought, she
reached over and kissed the baby.

"What is she called?" she asked.

Her mum looked at her smiling and said, "We thought you might help name her."

Gemma looked at the flowers, then she looked at the baby and said, "I'd like to call her Daisy."

"Daisy it is then," replied her mum, as she stroked Gemma's hair. "Then when she's older, she can help me out in our gran's garden." The thought of it made everyone smile.

THE END